ZAKIYA FATIN
ENTERPRISES

BOOK OF reminders

DAILY DOWNLOADS
TO RESET YOUR MIND

ZAKIYA FATIN

ZAKIYA FATIN
ENTERPRISES

Library of Congress Cataloging-in- Publication Data

Fatin, Zakiya
Book of Reminders

Daily downloads to reset your mind / Zakiya Fatin

Print ISBN: 978-1-09834-423-8
eBook ISBN: 978-1-09834-424-5

*This book is dedicated to my grandmother and my mother, Dorothy and Vanita Cruse, the wind beneath my wings.*

# *Preface*

Many people suffer in silence because they don't know how to heal. They don't know how to put back the broken pieces or find the missing parts of themselves they've lost along the way.

If you are one of those people, know you are not alone. We all have our personal struggles, challenges, and issues. Even those who show up the strongest, the brightest, and most resilient have things that they are dealing with, healing from, and moving through.

There have been times in my life that I have felt lost. Times that I had no hope, no vision for my life, and no clue what was next for me. I stopped giving myself permission to dream and to do the things that I loved to do. Anything that took me out of my comfort zone—anything that felt unsafe or caused a rise of fear within me—I absolutely would not do. I was already in too much pain. I had already experienced too much loss. The suffering and brokenness were more than I thought I could handle. In my mind I could not and would not recover from yet another disappointment, heartbreak, or failure.

I stopped trusting and believing in myself. I stopped believing that my life had any purpose beyond pain.

But here I am, confirming and testifying that there is something magical that happens when you live through what you thought you couldn't, when you survive the worst of the worse times of your life.

You may not realize it, or feel it, but you are so much more than what you think of yourself. You know more than you think you know, you are stronger than you believe yourself to be, and you have unaccessed knowledge and wisdom within you, waiting for an opportunity to present itself to the world and be put to use! I had to learn that life never stops! As long as there is breath in my body, I can count on rough times. I should expect to be challenged. You see, there will always be a different situation or circumstance in your life designed to stretch and grow you, and to prepare you for what's to come. But also know that you can trust that there will be ease, that you will find your joy and your purpose. You will grow through it all, you will learn through it all, and you will heal in the midst of it all!

This is a book of "reminders" that will support you in remembering the truth—your truth. As you read this book, give yourself permission to explore how these reminders apply to where you are in your life right now.

Take your time. Be open to what each reminder awakens, shifts, and triggers within you. Allow yourself to look beyond what's on the surface and go deeper.

This book will help you explore your willingness to take a deeper look at yourself and the areas in your life in which you are growing, learning, and forgiving.

In this book of reminders, you will find answers, resolutions, inspiration, guidance, and encouragement that support self-care, new awareness, forgiveness, and healing.

It is offered that you start this book from wherever you wish. For example, you may open the book to Reminder 26, which may be the reminder that speaks to or applies to a feeling, situation, or circumstance you are facing or dealing with right now. That reminder may be just what you need to start or end your day; it may be what you'll need tomorrow as you are moving about your day, and it may just very well be a message you can share with someone else. Be open to the possibility that this book will address everyday situations

2

and challenges you are moving through, to, or from. Allow yourself to experience fully what each reminder has the ability to heal in your life. Allow your engagement with each reminder to enrich your understanding of your path, your journey, life experience, and the endless possibilities it holds.

# Reminder #1

When you accept that it is what it is and that it was never what you thought or wanted it to be, then you start the process of moving on and letting go.

# Reminder #2

In the midst of brokenness, you will experience pain; in the midst of loss, you may wonder why. Although it doesn't feel like it, you are in the midst of growing; you are being stretched beyond the strength you know, the power you know, and the courage you know. Be open and trust that it is all working to make you a better you.

# Reminder #3

Do not be distracted by what was. Every new moment offers a new gift—don't miss it living in the past.

# Reminder #4

When you move into a new thing, don't ruin it by trying to attach, bring along, or hold on to the old stuff. Open your hands and let go of what no longer serves you!

# Reminder #5

How is being mad or angry supporting you? How is the bitterness you're holding on to affecting you? What would happen if you chose to let it all go? Think about it. You're still here, and you're still standing—in spite of it all. Remember how far you've come, remember what you've made it through, and remember who you are.

# Reminder #6

Put a plan together, commit to it, and execute it! The results will make you proud.

# Reminder #7

When you tell yourself the truth, it is in that moment that everything changes. It is in that moment that you take full responsibility and ownership over your life and your actions. When you tell yourself the truth, the stories you once told and the lies you once lived no longer have control over you.

# Reminder #8

Prove yourself wrong about you! Do what you keep telling yourself is impossible.

# Reminder #9

Position yourself to win. Drop the excuses and get to work!

# Reminder #10

Do for yourself what others won't. Do the things you are afraid to do and the things you've told yourself you cannot do. Push past what is uncomfortable, and be willing to step beyond the boundaries you've placed on yourself. When you do that, watch how many doors open for you, watch what you have the capacity and the courage to do, and watch how things get done—when you have the courage to believe in you.

# *Reminder* #*11*

Surrender wanting and needing to control how God handles it. It's absolutely none of your business how He gets it done. God's got it. Your job is to *trust*!!!

# Reminder #12

You'll think you know enough until you learn more.

You'll think you've had the best until you experience something better.

# Reminder #13

Forgive, forgive, forgive, and then forgive some more! Forgive yourself first so that you can than forgive others.

# Reminder #14

Be deliberate. Be intentional. Be committed to your own life, your own joy, your own journey, your own vision, and your own purpose. Stop being so quick to dive into someone else's vision for your life.

# Reminder #15

God knew what you would do. He knew how you would do it, when you would do it, and to whom you would do it. He knew what you would say, where you would go, and how you would end up. Whether you judge these things as good or bad, forgive yourself because God has already forgiven you. He knew the worst of the worse that you would do, and He created you anyway—there is still purpose for your life.

# *Reminder* #16

It's okay to not be okay. Feel hurt, get angry, even cry if you need to. Give yourself the opportunity to feel what you need to feel, and allow yourself the time and space you need to heal. You will recover.

# Reminder #17

It was necessary! All the loss, the hurt, the lies, the abuse, the choices, the misunderstandings, the abandonment, the violation, the disrespect, the broken heart, and the very thing you're going through right now were and are necessary!

Necessary to make you stronger.

Necessary to stretch you.

Necessary to grow you.

Necessary to teach you.

Necessary for you to learn to honor yourself, love yourself, and live with integrity.

Necessary to believe and trust yourself.

Necessary to teach you to tell the truth and be honest with yourself and others.

Necessary to show you how far you've come.

And the biggest of them all, necessary to bring you to this very moment, this moment of self-discovery, reliance, and surrender to God's will for your life. It was all necessary.

# Reminder #18

The truth robs the lie of its power! Tell the truth, free yourself, and release the burdens you've been carrying!

# Reminder #19

More!

Never stop searching for it.

Never stop seeking it.

Never stop expecting it.

Never stop trusting you can have it.

Never stop giving it.

Never stop recognizing when you have it.

More!

There is always more!

# Reminder #20

Stop acting like you don't know who you are! Whose you are and why you are! Someone's life depends on your greatness—take a breath and tighten up. You've got work to do!!!

# *Reminder #21*

Leaving is not losing, letting go is not failure, and stopping is not quitting.

They are all indications that you have surrendered, that you have grown, shifted, changed, and made a different choice for yourself.

# Reminder #22

Remain present; don't try to escape the moment. You cannot think away your feelings, you cannot run from them either.

They remain and affect you in other ways, even if you refuse to face them.

# Reminder #23

Try humility, vulnerability, flexibility, surrender, and trust. What do pride, ego, rigidness, and the need to control get you?

# Reminder #24

If you don't believe in the possibilities that today holds, go back and measure the weight of your burdens from yesterday.

# Reminder #25

They may have left you, but you walked out on you first. How have you abandoned yourself? How have you betrayed yourself? How have you done to yourself the things you are mad at others for doing to you?

# *Reminder* #26

Before you go off blaming someone for your current state, explore what you've allowed, how you've settled, what you've been doing, and how you've been doing it. Get clear about the story you've been telling yourself that has allowed the situation you face to exist in your life. How did you create it? What was your role in it? It's never about the other person; it's all always about you! Your growth, your healing, your stretch, your lesson.

# Reminder #27

It doesn't matter how much you've done, how much you've been there, or how much you've shown up for others. Don't hold the expectation that they will do the same, be the same, or show up the same way for you. Not everyone loves how you love or gives the way you give. Give without expectation, be who you are, and also know that there are some walks in life you will walk alone and some things you will do on your own. But don't worry—take a breath, gather yourself, and move forward.

# Reminder #28

The minute you realize that you are not the same person you were when you made that commitment, and that everything that once was has shifted and changed, you are not obligated to stay loyal to what no longer applies. You can change your mind. You still have a choice.

# Reminder #29

If you're asking how or why a person could do this to you or why they wouldn't do that for you, it's because they couldn't—they couldn't do it any differently than the way they did it. They couldn't say it any better than the way they said it, and they couldn't be for you anymore than they were. They were never taught, and just because you intellectually think they should know better doesn't mean they do. They did the best they knew how—right, wrong, or indifferent. Forgive them and forgive yourself for allowing it and move on.

# Reminder #30

Purpose: Find it! Stick with it! Live in it!

# Reminder #30

Don't assume you have tomorrow.

If there is something to be said, say it.

If there is something that needs to be done, do it.

If there are apologies to be made, make them.

If it's time to move, move.

Stop waiting! Do it right now! Stop wasting time!

# Reminder #31

Don't waste time doing things you know you have no business doing. It's a distraction from where your focus should be—on you!

# Reminder #33

You can spend your time making excuses, wanting more, wishing and hoping for more and for better, or you can spend your time doing what's required to get to what's next. The choice is yours.

# Reminder #34

Find your why, live your purpose, have your joy! It's all inside of you; stop looking outside of yourself for the answers.

# Reminder #35

I know you think you're lost. I know you think the sacrifices you've made and the time you spent were not recognized and were all for nothing. I know you're angry, feeling foolish, broken, and alone. The truth is, it's normal to feel all these things because you are losing something—you're losing the part of you that no longer serves you. You've sacrificed yourself over and over again, and now it's time to get back to you. In order to do that, you've got to lose some things and leave some people behind. You may even have to be walked out on, talked about, and maybe even beat down. But know this: you are being prepared for far greater things than the things you've lost or given up. Those opportunities you've missed, and the people you've left, were all part of the process. You are being readied to become the person you prayed to be. It's a bigger plan working than the one you see.

# Reminder #36

What you give, gives itself back to you. Check your results.

# Reminder #37

You don't have to have what others think is important in order to be valuable—especially if your values are different from theirs.

# Reminder #38

The good times don't expose who you are. It's the hard times that do. When you're being tested, the way you react or respond says a lot.

# Reminder #39

This is no show; it's your life. Don't entertain people's thoughts and ideas of who you are and who you are not. Don't put on a bootleg performance because you have an audience. Stand for something! Live for you! Be true to who you are! Be authentic!

# Reminder #40

Just because you behave badly doesn't mean you're bad. Hurt people sometimes hurt other people; when you know better, you do better. You do not have to go around hurting people. Do the work you need to do to heal, and ask for support if you need it. Take ownership for your actions.

# Reminder #41

Dream or vision? Know the difference. One requires nothing but sleep to achieve, while the other requires everything if you want it. Are you sleeping or are you awake?

# Reminder #42

When old thoughts, beliefs, stories, people, things, and ways present themselves, remind yourself and inform them that you have moved on and that you are not who you used to be.

# Reminder #43

You will have moments. Be present to them.

You will have memories. Appreciate them.

You will miss opportunities. Learn from them.

You will mourn the losses. Grieve them.

You will move beyond the hurt. Give yourself permission.

You will be more than you ever imagined you'd be. They're called blessings. Believe in them.

# *Reminder #44*

Not feeling anything today? It's really okay! Go back to bed! Tomorrow's a new day. Start over tomorrow! Take care of yourself.

# Reminder #45

Pay attention to the things you're okay with, the things you let slide, and the things you settle for. These things will let you know just how much you respect, value, appreciate, know, and take care of yourself. Once you see how you've been treating yourself, you will then understand how it's possible that others have treated you the exact same way! You teach people how to treat you by the way you treat yourself!

# Reminder #46

When God says there is no more waiting, there is no more procrastinating. When God says now, it doesn't matter whether you think you're ready. When God says now, it's now! The shift, the change, the lesson, the growth, the experience are happening now! Stop running from the now! The blessing is happening right now!

# Reminder #47

Ask God to give you a spirit of okay! This will help you accept what is. It will also allow you to do something about the things you can and make peace with the things you can't.

# Reminder #48

Forgiveness is for you. It doesn't mean what has been done or said to you is okay. It doesn't excuse the behaviors of others, and surely it doesn't make right what is wrong. You can, however, release the hurt, anger, rage, disappointment, bitterness, and brokenness. Being unwilling to forgive holds you hostage to unpleasant past experiences. Forgive so you can be free.

# Reminder #49

How you choose to respond and whom you choose to be in the midst of difficulty, challenging times, and struggles hold all the answers to why your experience is what it is. Check your first response—it holds all the answers.

# Reminder #50

Stop searching for something that's not there! If you don't see it, it's not there; if you don't hear it, it's not there; if you don't feel it, you can forget it—it isn't there. Stop holding on to the what if's. If someone changes for you, it'll only be for a little while. If you see the change, it'll only be a glimpse. If you can almost hear it, it still won't be quite it. If you tell yourself something is different this time, it's just a reflection of that lie you're telling yourself. It is not sustainable. The truth is what you wanted; it was never there. What you needed wasn't there either. The things you desired and deserved—you only got enough of to stay put. What you're looking for can never be found in places in which you settle or in places you know you don't belong. And surely it won't be provided externally through someone or something else. It can only be found in you. That's where you start. Give you what you need. What others bring to the table is a bonus.

# Reminder #51

Figure out what makes you happy and go with that. Get back to the basics—the simple things.

# *Reminder #52*

Pray! It lifts, elevates, inspires, and *changes things*! Make sure you're praying. Don't stop praying!

# Reminder #53

The moment you start to doubt or second-guess yourself, *stop*! Remind yourself of what you've been through, of how far you've come, and about the guts it took to get through what you've been through! That's your proof and all the evidence you need to get through what you're going through.

# Reminder #54

Focus on the positive. We put so much energy into the negative things. We focus on the negative. We recognize it and accept it, but the good things we overlook, ignore, forget quickly, and doubt. What if it was the other way around? What if you focused more on the positive, more on the blessings? How would you feel? Who would you be? What would you accomplish?

Remember that what you put your energy into is what flourishes in your life.

Focus on the good; recognize the good; make that your new habit and your new norm.

# Reminder #55

God sends what and who we need when we need it. He sends it when we are ready, open, available, and responsible enough for it. What shows up and who shows up is the answer you've been praying for!

# Reminder #56

Stay away from the things and the people that drain you mentally and emotionally. You simply aren't safe when you engage them. Your weakness for them is dangerous because you don't feel the impact of your interaction with them until after there's a disruption in your being.

# Reminder #57

Let today be the first best day of the rest of your life! It's never too late to start over. It's a choice.

# Reminder #58

Stop depending on people to encourage and inspire you. Don't give others the responsibility of validating your moves or supporting your dreams, accomplishments, and goals. Give yourself what you expect from others. Be for you what others refuse to be for you. You are your own responsibility.

# Reminder #59

Do more listening than talking! More feeling than thinking! More trusting than doubting. Have more faith than worry! Just start with today—it will make a difference.

# *Reminder* #60

Do not resist the things that have shown up in your life. If it's there, it's because you need it to grow. If it's lost, you no longer need it. If they left, it's because they could not stay—their purpose in your life was complete. If you feel lost, it's because you probably are. But don't worry. You're exactly where you need to be—learning what you need to learn. Be okay with what is and with what was, and get excited about what's coming!

# Reminder #61

There will be times in your life that you'll be tested with the very things you hold near and dear. When you are obedient to God's will and instructions, regardless of how tired you are, no matter how broken you feel, or how lost you seem to feel, the outcome will be favorable when you remain faithful—when you believe.

# Reminder #62

Whether you remember it or not, you used to have dreams and a vision for your life. You believed in the unseen, the unknown, and in the possibility that you could and would someday be standing in the midst of a reality that you once called a dream! Allow yourself to dream again, and never stop believing.

# Reminder #63

In every beginning there is truth—your truth which becomes the reality of your experience. In every start there is an end game, a vision, a focus, a finish. In every first step there is possibility—endless possibility. Don't be afraid to take the first step!

# Reminder #64

People are jealous and envious of you but have no idea what it takes to be you—the sacrifices you make, what it takes to smile every day, to push through, to grind, and to keep moving in spite of your own personal afflictions. If they knew what it takes to be in your position, to have your success, your money, or whatever it is they're jealous of, they'd fold when faced with the opportunity to walk in your shoes because they're not built for it! You are, and that's why you're in this position!

# Reminder #65

Just because the decision you're making is painful doesn't mean it's wrong. The pain will pass. Honor your choice.

# Reminder #66

In order for things to change, *you simply have to change*! You have to be different. You can no longer show up the way you've been showing up and doing the things you've been doing and expecting things to change. Do it different this time!

# Reminder #67

Your specialness—your genius—comes from you simply being you! Your gifts and talents are yours alone. Embrace them; never compromise or dummy down who you are because someone says, thinks, or feels you should!

# Reminder #68

It's not enough to just want more! You've got to put the work in for more!

# Reminder #69

Feel it and let it pass! Don't get stuck in the story you create about what you're feeling or what you're going through means.

# Reminder #70

Once you know the truth, you can't go back to not knowing. It doesn't work that way. You will suffer and lose every time you pretend to not know what you know.

# Reminder #71

Don't try to understand the things you can only survive. Some things aren't meant for understanding; they are designed for you to live through. You are stressed and angry because you are trying to understand and make sense of it all. Some things are none of your business. Surrender it, hand it over. Nothing is too big for God; He can handle it.

# Reminder #72

Get clear about who and what's worth fighting for. Once you know, fight like you've never fought before and let go of what's not worth fighting for. It will take intention, focus, discipline, and commitment, but never give up on the people or things that matter most to you.

# Reminder #73

If it's too much, slow down.

If it's too loud, stop talking.

If it's complete chaos, stop.

Breathe, be still, and wait.

You will get the instruction, the download, or the reminder.

Your gut will speak to you. No matter how the information comes, trust it. Don't make a move or decision a second before you have clarity! Sometimes the answer is to be still and do nothing.

# *Reminder* #74

The opportunity to change, be different, and do better is given on a moment-to-moment basis. You don't have to wait for your circumstances or your situation to change in order to make a change. Do it now; everything else will fall into place.

# *Reminder #75*

Focus, not on the other person but on yourself. Learn your lesson, own your part, and go apologize if needed.

# *Reminder* #76

Moving on is hard when you really don't want to, but it's necessary when you know you have to! Don't delay your departure. Staying a little longer won't change the fact that it's time to go.

# Reminder #77

When an idea strikes, and all of a sudden you can see it clearly through your mind's eye and there is excitement flowing through your body and it feels like it's happening now, that's when you know the time is now! Start the business, make the move, buy the house—whatever it is, now is the time. Take that leap of faith! Don't let fear stop you.

# Reminder #78

Be very careful about what you take on, accept, and deal with—especially if it's not yours in the first place!

# Reminder #79

When God starts to remove things or people from your life, how do you respond? How do you react? Do you get angry? Do you fall into a place of despair and hopelessness? Do you get still? Are you patient and trusting in His plan? Do you get excited because He's making room for something greater? Who do you become? All these things matter in the process of life. Pay attention to who you become and what you do when life presents itself.

# Reminder #80

Who you used to be or what you used to do doesn't matter or work for the person you are becoming. What worked before doesn't work now. New you. New method!

# Reminder #81

Let people know where you started so they understand your story. Invite them to see your journey, know your struggles, and feel your loss, your wins, your embarrassments, and your accomplishments so that they too believe and trust that there is more for them on the other side of what they are going through, moving through, pushing through, and pressing through! Share your journey!

# Reminder #82

What others have and what others are doing have nothing to do with you! What is for you is for you. What is going on in others lives does not stop anything from happening in your life, unless you stop your process to focus on theirs.

# Reminder #83

Sometimes you just have to sit in the reality and feel the pain of what you created—without blame, without guilt, without shame, but with acceptance. You are where you are; what's done has been done and you can't change it. What you can do is decide right now that this will not break you! This will not stop you! This does not change or devalue who you are and what you're created to do. You get to decide to let it go. Release the judgments and stories you're telling yourself about it. Free yourself, forgive yourself, and do better next time.

# Reminder #84

You don't have to know how; you just have to be willing! Willing to stretch, willing to learn, willing to move, willing to let go, willing to forgive, willing to be different, willing to be still, willing to hold on and wait, willing to trust, willing to love, willing to live! It is in your willingness that you create space for opportunity instead of stagnation.

# Reminder #85

The more time you spend wishing things were different, the less time you spend allowing and creating space for change to occur!

# Reminder #86

Allow yourself to experience something new today! Do a new thing—something you've never done before! Be creative! Stretch!

# Reminder #87

You have to understand that you may lose it all. That's the potential cost of gaining everything!

# Reminder #88

Do something and be something greater than yourself today.

# Reminder #89

Pain is pain, hurt is hurt, disappointment is disappointment.
How you hold it, what you do with it, and what you tell yourself
about it determines the amount of power it has over you!

# Reminder #90

If you want it, you've got to build it! That doesn't mean walking away because it's hard or uncomfortable. When things don't turn out or look the way you want them to, it's all still part of God's plan. You've got to build up the strength, the courage, the endurance, the will, the patience, the stamina, the faith, the trust, and the discipline if you want it!

Your relationship

Your business

Your health

Your career

Your peace

Your family

You've got to build it!

# Reminder #91

Chase after God.

Whatever he's saying to you, listen.

Whatever he's telling you to do, do.

Whoever he's calling you to be, be.

The message he's giving you, speak it.

Where he's taking you, follow.

He will never steer you wrong; there is always a greater plan in motion than the one you see.

# Reminder #92

When something begins to unravel and come undone, take a step back and let it happen. It will scare you. You will panic. You will become confused and maybe even angry. You may not understand or feel like you can survive. But sometimes it all has to come apart to be put back together. You can't stand on a foundation that's in pieces; it will not continue to carry you, you will eventually fall through the cracks.

# Reminder #93

Believe in the magic of a moment!
Everything can change in an instant! Be ready.

# Reminder #94

The biggest mistakes I've made were the ones I made when I ignored the conversation myself was trying to have with me. You always know what's best for you! Whether you want to accept it or not is up to you!

# Reminder #95

It's up to you! Where you go, who you become, what you say, and what you do are all up to you! The power is in your mind, your hands, your walk, and your talk. Who are you choosing to be or not to be? What will you build or destroy? What will you say and what will you keep to yourself? What parts of you will you let live, and what parts will you allow to die? It's up to you. It's all always been up to you.

## *Reminder #96*

Be grateful for God's promises. Don't forget the ways He has kept those promises. Whatever you are healing within yourself, whatever hardships you face, and however or wherever you end up, remember the promises of His word and stand on His word.

# Reminder #97

May your lowest place in life be the turning point that propels you forward; may it be the moment you realize, recognize, and reconsider your worth, your value, and your purpose. May you begin to reassure, reestablish, and reaffirm yourself within yourself.

# Reminder #98

Do not stop! If you keep going, you will arrive at the door of your greatest opportunity and accomplishment.

# Reminder #99

It's light work! It's not as deep or as heavy as you're making it!
Take a breath and start over.

# Reminder #100

Is it enough? Is what you're doing and who you're being enough? Check in and make sure it's enough!

# Reminder #101

Richness and wealth come from your life lessons and experiences. When you learn the lessons that the things in life come to teach you, you will begin to obtain all the riches and wealth the world has to offer.

# Reminder #102

Sometimes it just happens and you feel it on the inside. You feel something shift, change, or transform. You can't explain it, but you know your DNA is changing and your life will never be the same. Rest in this truth and use it to govern your thoughts, actions, and narrative, no matter what you are facing—good or bad, easy or hard, big or small. Know that you have all it takes to handle it.

# Reminder #103

Because you have no idea what your life is for!

Because you don't know what the trials you face are preparing you for!

Because you have no clue what your learning is about!

Because you can't foresee what tomorrow holds!

Focus on today—this moment, this second, this hour.

Realize that in the shortest second you can awaken.

In the quickest moment your life can change.

In a matter of minutes your purpose can be revealed.

And with just one deep inhale and exhale, it can and will happen!

# Reminder #104

I get it.

You're unsure.

You feel afraid.

You feel like you're lost.

You feel uncertain and unclear.

You feel stuck and bound.

You feel inadequate and hopeless and you just don't know.

Do it anyway. Go for it anyway.

How else will you know? How else will you grow? How else will you learn?

Do it! Go for it! Take a chance on you!

# Reminder #105

How do you know it's God and not you? That's the question most people ask. Find a place. The place you go where you can be still, where you can quiet the noise of the day-to-day dealings and the demands, wants, needs, and expectations of others, the place you go to quiet the noise of your mind. It is in this space that you make yourself available to hear and receive guidance, instruction, clarity, and the answers you've been seeking. It is in this space you can hear God.

# *Reminder* #*106*

When someone or something shows up, the *whys* are not always clear. Don't fall into trying to adjust your vision to get a clear picture or understanding. Be still and know that with time it will all become clear. Patience. Practice patience.

# Reminder #107

You win some, you lose some. The loss builds you; the win certifies you!

# Reminder #108

Don't be sold on short moments in time.

Don't buy into what's being sold if you have no proof that it's real.

When the proof is there, when you know that you know beyond a shadow of a doubt—it's those moments that change your life.

# Reminder #109

What is regular to you is exceptional and extraordinary to someone else.

What you consider a waste of time is time well spent to another.

What you view negatively is all a person needs to positively grow.

What you see as a loss, someone else sees as an opportunity to learn and get it right the next time.

What you think is a closed door is open for someone that knows all they have to do is turn the knob and walk through it or kick it open.

You have allowed the circumstances, the hardships, the pain, and the suffering to break you, but someone else has taken that same circumstance, hardship, pain, or suffering and used it as motivation. The point is, you and your life are entirely up to you!

# Reminder #110

You cannot fix something that's finished. When it's over, it's over; when it's done, it's done. The more you insist on breathing life into something that is dead is how you enter into a practice of self-betrayal. Leave it dead so that you can live the life you truly desire.

# Reminder #111

Don't allow people to project their stuff on to you. Don't allow people to dictate your mood, how you move about in your life, or how you feel about yourself. If you are allowing these things, you are giving your power away and giving them control over you. Stop doing that!

# Reminder #112

Some people are invested in a version of you that no longer exists. They will be mad at you for not remaining the same broken, wounded, lost, and dependent person. You see, who you used to be fulfilled a purpose for them, and now that you've taken that away, they no longer know where or how they fit in your world. The great thing about this is that one of two things will happen: they will adjust or they will get as far away from you as possible. All you have to do is stay true to who you are and watch the beauty of your life unfold!

# Reminder #113

If you drop all the titles, leave off all the degrees, and stop being the person the world sees, who then would you be? The freedom you seek is in your answer to this question.

# Reminder #114

Are you ready for what you've been praying for? Can you handle the responsibility it will require you to step into? Will you make the sacrifices it asks of you? How will you handle the changes it demands from you? God answers prayers, and prayer changes things! So pray and prepare!

# Reminder #115

You may be a product of your environment. You may have lost some things. You may have experienced some hard and unthinkable things. You may feel trapped and caged in your own mind, but none of that can take away your gift and your ability to fly. You will be unstoppable the moment you decide to stop letting fear and discomfort and old habits stop you.

# Reminder #116

It is what it is! The fact that you call it or see it as something different doesn't change what it is. This is called acceptance.

# Reminder #117

Your life's curriculum—this journey you're on—was divinely constructed and designed to make you the master of your thoughts, your actions, your beliefs, your behavior, and your life.

## Reminder #118

When it's over, it's over. When it's done, it's done. When it's finished, it's finished. Stop trying to resuscitate what's already dead. Stop trying to squeeze yourself into places you don't fit in. Stop holding on to people who let you go a long time ago. Stop doing what doesn't work.

# Note from the Author

Live your life to its fullest! Be brave, be courageous, and be unapologetically you!

You deserve all the amazing things you desire, and you can have them all.

Do the work required to heal. Always do your best and be your best.

Remember that there is always a bigger picture operating than the one you see. Never limit yourself, never doubt yourself and don't abandon yourself. Love yourself, trust yourself, honor yourself, and be yourself instead.

*Sakiya Fati*

# Other Books

As children, preteens, and young adults, there are so many things we go through, endure, and experience. These things can be confusing and hard, but can also be things that are often fun, liberating, and exciting, and sometimes, things that are hurtful, life changing, and unfair. This book of "Reminders" is filled with information, answers, encouragement, and things to remember as you journey and navigate through your life.

This book will give you clarity, guidance, and understanding, while reminding you, that you have the strength, courage, and drive to get through the situations, experiences, and things you may face.

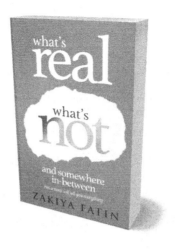

So many of us women have been through so much with our men. We could in our minds legitimately say they took advantage of us. Undoubtedly, we could feel and believe in our hearts they disrespected, devalued, diminished, disrupted, and disassociated themselves from our lives. Some of us could say, "He is the absolute best thing that's ever happened to me." It really just depends on where you are in your life's journey and your relationship with men. This is a book of reminders, and information, that will support you with things you may have forgotten, never learned, and find completely confusing about the men or man in your life.

This book will bring to life the wisdom of your deepest thoughts, knowings, and understanding—provoking and confirming things you already know, things from which you've been running from acknowledging, or accepting about the situations you are facing or have experienced in your relationships.

How would you feel if you knew, it was all necessary? Every new and exciting beginning, every disappointing and hard ending, even the struggle you may be facing right now of trying to decide to stay or leave, every loss and every gain—it was all necessary for you to stretch, learn, grow, and evolve.